بِسْمِ اللهِ الرَّحْمٰنِ الرَّحِيمِ

ERTUGRUL GHAZI
A Very Short Biography

Crescent Books

Praise for
Ertugrul Ghazi

Flamur's critical work on the life of Ertugrul depicts the spirit of the man who paved the way for the rise of the House of Osman. It tells the true story of a hero and his tribe that embodied elements of great character based on unshakable faith and bravery...It is an inspiring account for all generations to come.

— **Imam Burhan Al Din Fili**, author of *Hope is Alive*

The Turkish drama about Ertugrul Ghazi has been popular globally for several years, but most viewers do not know about this great warrior›s life and personality. This short biography beautifully fills that void.

— **Prof. Dr. Amber Haque**, co-author of *Psychology of Personality*

Many of us who enjoy a good book are making the best of these troubling times by venturing further afield to find gems in the form of written words. And few sparkle more than *Ertugrul Ghazi: A Very Short Biography* by Flamur Vehapi, an excellent researcher and writer. Vehapi takes readers on a fascinating trip into 13th century Turkey where Ertugrul was an important tribal leader and father of Osman, founder of the Ottoman empire. It is an interesting read that broadens your historical horizons.

— **Paul Fattig**, author of *Madstone*

At last someone has resurrected the long-forgotten life story of the person who gave rise to a global empire... A refreshing and captivating account.

— **Prof. Dr. Naser Bresa**, author of *Retrospektiva*

Ertugrul Ghazi is a looming figure in Turkish and Islamic history. The more we learn of his life and accomplishments the more we appreciate what he has achieved but more importantly the strength of his character and convictions. We are inspired through Ertugrul›s example to fight for our and our community›s well-being, honor, and highest aspirations while always steadfastly maintaining our moral compass. This well researched, short, yet succinct biography does just that. Turkish Bork hats off to Flamur. Today he has raised the Kayi flag just a little higher.

— **Brandon Mayfield**, author of *Improbable Cause*

It was an absolute delight to watch the 448 episodes [of 'Resurrection'] about the life and legacy of Ertugrul. The hundreds of hours we spent viewing the series was a great bonding and empowering experience for our family. The millions of people who enjoyed and seemed "addicted" to the drama did so because the characters of the show resonated with their core values, especially the pursuit of justice and mercy. Next to the example of our beloved Prophet Muhammad *pbuh*, the prophets, and the righteous companions, Ertugrul is another historical figure worth knowing...Flamur continues to impress me with his search for beauty around the world and throughout history, and I am glad he helped us resurrect the story of Ertugrul.

— **Dr. Omar Reda**, author of
On the Shoulders of the Prophet

The story of the obscure historical figure Ertugrul came to life for most people with the globally popular Turkish TV series *Diriliş: Ertuğrul* (Resurrection: Ertugrul). Now Flamur offers us a scholarly insight into the historical figure of Ertugrul, the father of Osman who was the founder of the Ottoman dynasty[1] that ruled an empire for more than six hundred years. I am glad to recommend this book that timely provides the reader with a concise scholarly biography of the forgotten Turkic nomad warrior who gave rise to a world empire.

— **Assoc. Prof. Dr. Amjad H. Hussain**, author of *A Social History of Education in the Muslim World*

ERTUGRUL GHAZI
A Very Short Biography

by
Flamur Vehapi
with a Foreword by Dr. Stef Keris

Crescent Books

First Published in 2021
by Crescent Books
an imprint of Crescent Institute LLC, Portland, OR

Prepared and Typeset
by Elipse Productions

ISBN: 978-1-954935-00-6
1. Ertugrul   2. Byzantines   3. Mongols
4. Crusaders   5. Sultan Alaeddin   6. Ottomans
7. Turkmen

First edition
Includes biographical references and appendices
Cover design by Erzen Pashaj
Cover art by © Ferhat Akil
Inside portrait by © Lama Bayoun

Printed in the United States of America

For my beloved
Suhail and Ryanne

FOREWORD

WHEN I WAS APPROACHED BY FLAMUR TO WRITE A FOREWORD for his book about Ertugrul, I felt honored. It was finally about time for the English-speaking world to find out more about the person who brought his tribe to Asia Minor and who raised the founder of the Ottoman Empire, Osman.

Although it is very difficult to find accurate information about Ertugrul, this brief work managed to present the facts, based on well-researched sources. I am very happy to see that original sources are used and authentic material has been uncovered for this extremely important research.

Seeing that the world is nowadays discovering the Ottomans and their history, it is important to look deeper into the beginning of such an empire. The famous series 'Resurrection: Ertugrul' has won hearts and souls even amongst the non-Muslims and has raised interest about Ottoman history. Well done! Enjoy this booklet!

With Islamic greetings,
Your Greek brother in Islam

Dr. Stef Keris, author of *The Islamic History of Europe*

Contents

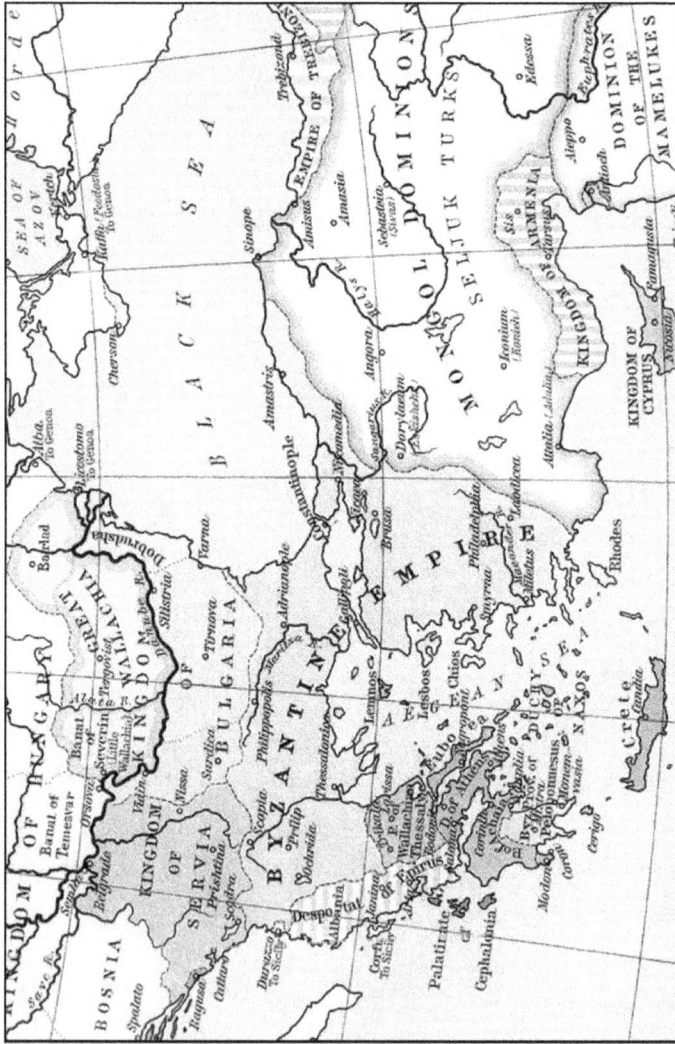

Fig. 1. The Byzantine Empire and Mongol control over Anatolia in 1265.[2]

Ertugrul's Path

By Burhan Al Din Fili[a]

From the lands of the east, a tribe went west,
seeking prosperity and not conquest.
Helped by the winds of faith, in Anatolia they arrived,
with optimism, and hard work they thrived.

Led by Gunduz Alp with faith and wisdom,
from land to land they sought freedom.
Their tent was the castle and school,
their proper upbringing was the main tool.

With the light of *iman* their life was furnished,
his son Ertugrul was properly nourished.
At the school of *RasulAllah*[b] was educated,
to the ranks of nobility was elevated.

On his father's path he proudly went on,
led by the light of his true *iman*.
He fiercely fought in three fronts:
The Mongols, Crusaders and the hypocrites' plots.
By Allah's grace and his strategy,
He brought to an end their tyranny.

For the great future he strived at his best,
his son Osman completed the rest.
Leading to the foundation of a great empire,
Ertugrul's vision never ceases to inspire.

---

[a] Fili is a renowned Muslim American poet from Albania, and the author of numerous books. His work has been translated into a number of languages, 2020.

[b] I.e., the Prophet Muhammad *pbuh.*

NOTE ON USAGE AND TRANSLITERATION

Almost all of the Ottoman and pre-Ottoman records we have access to are in Ottoman Turkish; that is the old Turkish language used in areas controlled by the Ottoman Empire from its inception until the adoption of the Roman alphabet in 1928 by the Turkish nationalist government. Prior to the formation of the modern Turkish Republic, Ottoman Turkish was written in Arabic script (as well as, but less often, in Hebrew, Greek, Armenian and other alphabets). Regardless of the script or language, many of the sources I have referred to here are as they have come down to us in modern Turkish.

As for the modern Turkish alphabet and the conversion/transliteration of Turkish sounds and letters, see *Appendix A* I developed at the end of this book. Those familiar with translation and the transliteration process, know that imposing an entirely consistent system for terms, names and places is almost impossible. For an easier read, however, almost all of the Ottoman/Turkish name spellings in this book have been anglicized, and the original spellings are included on their first mention. For instance, *Kayı* is spelled as Kayi, or *Ertuğrul* as Ertugrul after their first mention. Italics are used for non-English and technical terms such as *iman* or *ummah* only when the term is used for the first time, many of which are also included in the *Glossary of Terms, Names, and Places* at the end of the book. As for the Arabic terms, for the most part, I have adopted the spellings from the *Cambridge History of Islam* where indication of vowel length is often omitted. For place-names such as cities or regions, where there exists an accepted English name for it, that has been preferred, but the original is also given in parenthesis, i.e., Aleppo (Halep) or Izmir (İzmir). This rule does not apply to the footnotes and endnotes, however, since all of those are kept as given in their original sources.

Finally, I understand that too many footnotes can be distracting, for that reason, I have moved all footnotes (with citations only) to the end of the document as endnotes, footnotes with comments or explanations are left at the end of the page.

ABBREVIATIONS

AH	*anno Hegirai* meaning Hijrah (Islamic) year or After Hijrah
Ar.	Arabic
ca.	*circa* meaning about, approximately
c.	century
CE	Common Era
cf.	*confer* meaning compare
d.	died
ed.	editor or edited by
e.g.	for example
Eng.	English
ibid.	*ibidem* meaning in the same place
n.d.	no date
n.p.	no place
pass.	*passim* meaning found here and there or spread throughout
pbuh	peace be upon him, honorific used after the names of the prophets
r.	ruled or reigned
r.a.	May God be pleased with him
sic	*sic erat scriptum* meaning thus was it written
Tr.	Turkish
vol.	volume

INTRODUCTION

HE PERSONA OF ERTUGRUL (ERTUĞRUL) HAS GONE MOSTLY unnoticed outside the Turkish-speaking world. Many know of the Byzantine, Crusader, and Mongol leaders who occupied or ruled Anatolia, but not of the Kayis and their charismatic leader who relentlessly stood against such powers. Unlike those medieval powers, however, this group was a much smaller one. Ertugrul, after all, was only the head of a nomadic group of people among many other Turkmen tribes of no major significance in the region, at least for some time.

Those familiar with the history of medieval Anatolia, are certainly well aware of the Ottomans and many of their sultans, some of whom had pronounced relations with non-Muslims and others who wanted nothing to do with them. Numerous historians have recorded in detail the successes of the Ottomans and their later failures.[3] What most have failed to note is that the Ottomans did not swiftly rise to power in a vacuum. Thus, I would contend that the role of Ertugrul and the Kayis in the formation of the Ottoman (Osmanlı) Empire should not be overlooked. It was, in fact, the painstaking struggles of Ertugrul and of his *alps*[a] that resurrected the identity of a people which later led to the birth of a global empire. The following pages, which do little justice to those lengthy endeavors, will attempt to show how the actions of a few would forever change the course of history, at least for the region in question.

Reading the following accounts, however, one will notice that details on Ertugrul, this legendary leader, as well as his tribe are scant. In fact, most of the information we have about Ertugrul has come to us through later chronicles from the first Ottoman century.[4] That being the case, I have refrained from much interpretation of the events or characters mentioned in this book until further evidence might come to light. The majority of my sources for this book are in English, and as such, most of them provide a Western lens, though I have also consulted a number of Turkish sources in an effort to balance that.[5] I hope you enjoy reading these humble paragraphs as much as I enjoyed researching them.

---

[a] Alp or Alper, often used interchangeably, is a masculine given name and has two different but closely related meanings: a) hero, brave one, chivalrous, etc., and b) soldier.

WHO WAS ERTUGRUL?

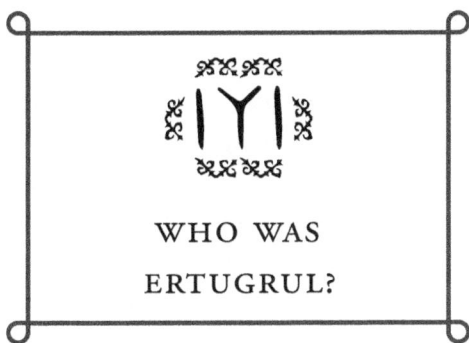

And put your trust in God, and enough is
God as a disposer of affairs.

— Qur'an 33:3

RTUGRUL GHAZI, ALSO KNOWN AS ERTUGRUL BEY, was a thirteen-century Muslim Oghuz Turkic leader from western Anatolia (the lands between the Black Sea, the Aegean, and the Mediterranean).[a] Ertugrul is said to have been born at the end of the 12th century CE, and he was the leader of his Kayi tribe for a great portion of his adult life.[b] He was known

---

[a] Although the term *ghazi* (or *gazi* in modern Tr.) is often used as an honorific title for a Muslim warrior, champion or hero, it originally referred to individuals who participated in *ghazwa*, meaning military campaigns against non-Muslims. The term was applied in early Islamic history to expeditions led by the Prophet Muhammad *pbuh*. Later, the term was used by Turkic leaders to describe their campaigns of conquest.

[b] Despite the fact that Ertugrul's date of birth is largely unknown, 1191 and 1198 are some of the dates I have come across for this event.

for his great valor, chivalry, military strategy, and justice—and most importantly, for his deep commitment to his faith and the well-being of his community. His life goal was to unite the *ummah*[a] as well as establish a homeland for the Turkic people who at that point were scattered throughout Asia Minor, the Middle East, and beyond. Although greatly outnumbered, inadequately equipped, and poorly positioned (i.e. sandwiched between two global forces, the Byzantines and the Mongols), Ertugrul and his superior warriors known as alps, challenged the superpowers of their time.[b] These warriors accomplished this while at the same time trying to secure peace with the competing local tribes and the rivaling Muslim empires in the region which were in total disarray at this point.[c] Ertugrul died in 1280 CE in Sogut (Söğüt) in present-day Turkey.[d] He left behind three sons, one of them being Osman I, known to us as the founder of the Ottoman dynasty.

---

[a] For this and other terms, see *Glossary of Terms, Names, and Places* at the end of this book.

[b] One particular alp, worthy of mention here is Turghut Alp. Turghut is said to have fought with Ertugrul until the latter passed away. He then served under Sultan Osman I as a military commander, and later under Sultan Orhan, the son of Osman. Turghut is said to have lived over 120 years. In honor of Turghut, there is a town in the Manisa Province in Turkey called Turgutalp (Tezcan, *The Second Ottoman Empire...*, 85-86, 2010. Cf. Şimşiroğlu, *Kayı I*, 2013).

[c] I.e. the remnants of the Ayyubids in Syria and the Seljuks in Anatolia.

[d] Due to historical gaps and discrepancies, the exact dates of Ertugrul's birth and death are difficult to confirm but some sources also indicate 1281 CE as the year when Ertugrul passed away.

The World Before and During Ertugrul's Time

So verily, with hardship, there is relief.

— Qur'an 94:5

THE GOLDEN AGE OF MUSLIM CIVILIZATION BEGAN SHORTLY after the passing of the Prophet Muhammad *pbuh* and the age of the Rashidun Caliphate. This was a truly revolutionary period since a great deal of learning, translating, as well as invention and discovery took place in the Muslim world. People from all parts of the medieval world, faiths, and backgrounds traveled to study at its centers of learning and contributed to this great civilization that was growing and flourishing right in front of their eyes.[6]

During this vibrant period, in addition to their own contributions, Muslim thinkers and scientists assimilated and further developed the ideas and the scientific knowledge of the civilizations they had overpowered. This included the works of the Greeks and Romans as well as those of the Persians, Egyptians, Indians, Chinese, and others. They further advanced the fields of education, biology, chemistry, medicine, algebra, geometry, calculus, and many more.[7] This was the age of influential scholars, scientists, artists, and philosophers like Imam Ahmad ibn Hanbal (780 - 855), Al Zahrawi or Abulcasis (936 - 1013), Ibn al-Haytham or Alhazen (965 - 1040), Ibn Sina or Avicena (980 - 1037), Ibn Rushd or Averroës (1126 - 1198) and others.

By the mid-thirteenth century, however, this leading civilization experienced a serious decline due to a number of factors primarily due to external invasions that resulted in bloodshed, destroyed infrastructure and resources, and disrupted people's ways of life.[a] This was the period of the Mongol conquests, who by this time had overrun most of Eurasian lands including much of the old Islamic caliphate.[8]

It was during these darkest of days in Muslim history— with Crusader armies invading Muslim lands on one side, and Mongol incursions pillaging and destroying Muslim livelihoods on the other—that Ertugrul Ghazi was born and raised. As circumstances dictated, Ertugrul's development and training centered around conflict, migration, hunting and combat training and shaped him into the leader he would become. In 1258, while the Mongols were wreaking havoc in the region, Ertugrul's son Osman was born. [9]This year coincided with the devastating Siege of Baghdad under the rule of Hulagu Khan (1218-1265) the grandson of Genghis Khan (1162-1227).

During this siege, the Mongols destroyed one of the greatest cities of the Muslim world along with all its knowledge and heritage and, depending on the source, killed between two hundred thousand to more than a million Muslims.[10] So great was the calamity on the ummah that the Muslim scholar, Ibn Katheer (1301-1373), wrote:

> *They [the Mongols] attacked the country and killed everyone they found of the men, women, children and elderly. Many people hid in wells, rubbish bins and*

---

[a] The date often used to mark this decline is 1258 CE. Year 1492 is also cited for this event which marks the completion of the Christian Reconquista of the Emirate of Granada in Al-Andalus.

grasslands for days; while others grouped together and locked themselves inside shops and mosques, but the Tatars broke in, by demolishing the doors or burning the fronts, and once inside, they chased the fleeing residents; slaughtering them on the roofs. None escaped from the massacre, except for Jews, Christians and those who had sought their protection.[11]

Although Osman's descendants would later reclaim those lands, this was the chaotic world Ertugrul and his children inherited—a world of great trials and tribulations.[12]

The Origins of the Turkic Nomads

O humanity, indeed We have created
you from a male and a female and made
you peoples and tribes so that you
may know one another.

— Qur'an 49:13

RTUGRUL'S ANCESTORS CAME FROM THE EURASIAN STEPPE where nomadic peoples inhabited the area for centuries.[a] These were pastoral communities living in tents who periodically moved in search of pastures more suitable for their grazing animals or to avoid some kind of conflict, or to find a better place for themselves.[13] During the eighth century, some of these tribes that migrated west were collectively referred to as the *Oghuz* people;[b] they had settled in western Central Asia.[14]

During this period, a new world order was being established—the age of the expansion of Islam with the rise of the Umayyad

---

[a] For this specific group of tribes, the area included lands from the borders of China across Turkestan and beyond (Kinross, *The Ottoman Centuries*, 1977). Cf. Yorulmazoglu, *The Turks* (vol. 1), 2017.

[b] The Oghuz were a group of western Turkic tribes that spoke the Oghuz branch of the Turkic language family. Findley notes that the Ughuz were a "confederation of twenty-odd clans or subtribes among which the Kinik ranked first and the Kayi(gh) second" (50, 2005). *Oghuz* is a Common Turkic word for 'tribe.'

and Abbasid dynasties. In fact, less than a century after the death of the Prophet Muhammad *pbuh* in 632 CE, Islam and Muslims had reached Spain and Portugal in the west and lands all the way to Pacific Ocean in the east.[15] Although the Turkic nomads were no match for the vigor of the new caliphate in the region, at least initially, they did establish reliable trade relations with the Muslim communities they came in contact with.[16]

Due to close interactions with Muslims, during the ninth century and onward, many of the nomadic tribes began to renounce their pagan beliefs and embrace Islam.[17] Thereupon, Muslim leadership recognized the values and martial qualities of the Turkmen[a] and began to recruit them into their ranks. "Apart from such moral values as endurance, self-discipline, and foresight, the nomadic way of life had bred in them a combative spirit, the habit of mobility, equestrian skills, and an unusual dexterity as archers on horseback" writes Scottish historian, Lord Kinross, when describing many of these Turkic tribes.[18]

As the Abbasid sphere of influence began to wane over time, a great deal of the Muslim military, including leadership roles were being held by the Turkmen to the point where in the eleventh century a group of Turkic nomads had established a dynasty of their own known [19] As the Seljuks, and other Turkic tribes, were establishing themselves in Asia Minor, however, there was not much resistance from the Byzantines. At this point, their populations were already overburdened and weakened by corruption, internal and external conflict, depletion of the agricultural labor force due to recruitment for fighting, heavy taxation.[20] It is also important to note here that the Seljuks quickly gained great respect in the region due to their successful campaigns against their rivals.[21]

---

[a] During the tenth century and onward, Islamic sources began referring to these Turkic tribes as Muslim Turkmen (Zachariadou, "Turkomans", 1991).

Under the leadership of Tughrul (Tuğrul) Bey (r. 1037-1063),[a] for instance, the Seljuks conquered all of Iran in 1054, and a year later, they entered Baghdad and ordered the Abbasid caliph to recognize Turghul Bey as the sultan and temporal ruler of the Muslim state.[22] In 1071, the Seljuk armies under the leadership of Alp Arslan (r. 1063 -1072), an esteemed figure in Seljuk history, defeated a Byzantine army and captured the Eastern Roman emperor at the Battle of Manzikert (Malazgirt).[23] This achievement boosted the Seljuk morale and undermined Byzantine authority in Anatolia, and it also opened the way for more Turkic tribes to move into Asia Minor.[24] Often referred to as "the worst disaster to befall Byzantium," the defeat at Mansiker caused such a setback for Christendom that it later provoked Pope Urban II to launch the First Crusade.[25]

Future generations of Turkic nomad children, throughout the lands of Anatolia and beyond, grew up with these stories of struggle, hope and victory. They learned how their leaders like Alp Arslan had captured the Byzantine emperor and decimated his army, how Suleiman ibn Qutalmish (Kutalmış, also known as Suleiman I)[b] established an empire of his own, and how a young commander like Kilij (Kılıç) Arslan, Suleiman's son, faced the first Crusaders and defeated many of their armies.[c] These narratives of valor and sacrifice enkindled their people's spirits of heroism and warriorship for centuries to come. The Kayi boys and girls must certainly have been told these stories and raised with such mores.

---

[a] Tughrul Bey was the founder of the Seljuk Empire.

[b] Qutalmish is also referred to at times as 'Qutalmish Suleiman Shah' and this may be where the confusion came regarding the name of Ertugrul's father, Gunduz Alp.

[c] Kilij Arslan I is said to have been the second leader of the Seljuks of Rum and the first of Muslim commanders to face the first Crusader army (Küçüksipahioğlu, "The First Turkish Leader against the Crusaders: Sultan Kilij Arslan," 63–83, 2015; Maalouf, *The Crusades through Arab Eyes*, 3-18, 1984).

The Kayis and the Others in the Region

All of the people are the children of Adam,
and Adam was created from dust.

— Prophet Muhammad *pbuh*

E DO NOT KNOW MUCH ABOUT ERTUGRUL'S LIFE, TRIBE or family, primarily because he and his family came from a tribe of nomads and not much of their history was written down. As is often the case, nomad culture is an oral culture, not a written one. That which was written was rare and often destroyed during conflict, lack of preservation or time itself, among other factors.[26] However, this lack of sources providing an inside glimpse of this time period and the people who lived there, cannot prevent us from appreciating just what the Turkic people as a whole managed to accomplish during this time, notes Rudi Lindner, adding that

The Seljuks and their occasional allies, the Turkmen nomads, had appropriated the plateau, taken over the management of its towns, and spread animal husbandry further among its fields. The introduction of Seljuk silver currency and the construction of the first urban mosques and rural caravansaries in the later twelfth century point toward a growth in trade and patronage.[27]

During the reign of Sultan Alaeddin Keyqubad I (r. 1220-1237), most nomadic tribes prospered militarily as well as financially.[28] Under direct Seljuk leadership, they "broke through Byzantine defenses in the north and south and gained outlets to the sea at Antalya and Sinope, whence trade became possible as far west as Venice and as far north as the Crimea."[29]

One such tribe that quickly rose to power and prominence was the Kayi tribe. There were a number of Turkic tribes in Anatolia during the time of Ertugrul, but the Kayi seems to have been one of the most influential playing a major role in the conquest, settlement, and expansion of Muslim dominion in western Anatolia. No other tribe is said to have come close to the achievements of the Kayis.[30] The Kayi, like the other tribes, was made up of a number of clans and the family of Ertugrul is said to have been from the Karakeçili clan of the Kayı tribe. [31]

Ertugrul's Family

No one who severs the ties of kinship
will enter Paradise.
— Prophet Muhammad *pbuh*

ERTUGRUL CAME FROM HUMBLE BEGINNINGS BUT WAS BLESSED with a prodigious family and a close-knit and supportive community as was often, and still is, the case in tribal societies. Ertugrul's father, Gunduz Alp (Gündüz Alp),[a] and his mother (whose name is often cited as Hayme Hatun or Hayme Ana)[32] had three other sons: Sungur Tegin, Gundogdu (Gündoğdu), and Dundar (Dündar). It is unclear if the couple had any daughters.

As for Ertugrul's wife, her name is often given as Halime Hatun or Halime Sultan, however, there is no conclusive evidence on her name or origins.[b] There is a grave located in the garden of Ertugrul's burial place in Sogut that bears her name but its historical authenticity has been disputed. [33] What we know is that Ertugrul and his wife had three sons, Savci (Savcı),[c] Gunduz (Gündüz), and Osman, the latter known as the founder of the Ottoman dynasty. [34]

---

[a] His name is also found as Gök Alp, but some sources indicate that Gök Alp was Gündüz Alp's brother.

[b] The term *hatun* was used as an honorific for women of a certain status, and it is roughly equivalent to the English term 'lady.'

[c] Savci's name is also found as Saru Batu Savcı Bey but there are some who claim that Saru Batu was another son of Ertugrul (a fourth one), however, no Ottoman sources confirm such counterclaim.

$$\Leftrightarrow\!\!\xi\!\!-\!\!3\!\!\Leftrightarrow$$

Ertugrul's Life and Times

Life consists of two days, one for you,
one against you. When it›s for you
don`t be proud or reckless, and when
it`s against you be patient, for both
days are a test for you.

— Ali ibn Abi Talib *r.a.*

E KNOW THAT ERTUGRUL WAS THE SON OF GUNDUZ ALP from the Kayi tribe of Oghuz Turks.[a] In fact, coins minted during the reign of Osman I read "Osman bin Ertuğrul bin Gündüz Alp" (from Ar. meaning Osman, son of Ertugrul, son of Gündüz Alp) indicating that the name of Ertugrul's father was Gunduz Alp.[35] We also know that Ertugrul was raised and educated in a religious family and was mentored by eminent scholars of his time. From an early age, his family instilled high morals and values in Ertugrul, and their other sons, a custom the Kayis seem to have practiced with their children for generations.[36] For example, before passing away, Ertugrul

---

[a] Some sources note that Ertugrul's father's name was Süleyman or Süleyman Shah but most modern historians have disputed this claim and have pointed out that this name, Süleyman Shah, was incorrectly attributed to him later on (Cf. Yilmaz, "Osmanlıların Kuruluşuna...," 8-38, 2015; İnalcık, "Osmanlı Beyliği'nin Kurucusu Osman Beg," 480-490, 2007).

did not have much from this world to bequeath to his sons but what he left them with was something much more valuable than earthly possession. He left them the company of the scholars and the love of spiritual knowledge to the point where Ertugrul's last will to his son, Osman, was to respect his teacher and mentor, Shaykh Edebali (1206-1326), learn from and never oppose him.[a] "Oppose me, oppose him not" said Ertugrul, and "If you oppose me, I will be sad and hurt. If you oppose him, my eyes will not look at you, even if they look they will not see ... Consider what I have said as my last will."[b]

At some point in the thirteenth century during the Seljuk period, Gunduz Alp and his followers left their homeland in Central Asia and settled their tribe in the eastern province of Bitlis in Anatolia near the historic town of Ahlat.[37] They had abandoned their homelands due to harsh terrains and poor climate in hopes of a more suitable life for themselves and their livestock.[c] Although thirteenth-century Anatolia itself is said to have been a land of great wealth, this move proved to be a challenging transition for the Turkic settlers.[38]

After various Mongol attacks in Anatolia, many of the Turkic tribes were pressured to migrate again to various places in the region.[39] The family of Ertugrul had moved toward Erzurum. However, according to Turkish historian, Erhan Afyoncu, when Gunduz Alp passed away and Ertugrul became the leader of his

---

[a] Shaykh Edebali, also known as Balışeyh, was an influential Ottoman Sunni theologian from the Arab Banu Tamim tribe. Edebali enjoyed great respect among his people and is known as one of the shapers and developers of Ottoman policies in the region during the rule of Osman I, the first Ottoman sultan. Osman later married Edebali's daughter (İnalcık, *The Ottoman Empire*, 55, 1973).

[b] Excerpt from Ertugrul's letter to Osman I found today on an engraved stone in the garden of Ertugrul's grave in Sogut, Turkey.

[c] Today, Anatolia makes up the majority of modern-day Turkey.

people, Ertugrul's older brothers, Sungur Tegin and Gundogdu returned to their father's original settlement in eastern Anatolia. Ertugrul and his younger brother, Dundar, moved west and settled in the Sivas-Tokat territories in the mid-Black Sea region of Anatolia.[40] It is said that the Kayi leader had about one hundred families with him and a little over four hundred horsemen,[41] all of whom were ready to give up their lives at the orders of their leader, as was often the case with many tribal societies.

The year 1230 seems to have been a turning point for the Kayis. That year, Ertugrul and his cadre of alps had come across a battle between the Seljuks and one of their enemy armies. Ertugrul and his alps had assisted Sultan Alaeddin Keykubad (r. 1220-1237) of the Anatolian Seljuks against their enemy.[42] This was probably a Byzantine army but it could have also been Mongol, or even of the Khwarezm Shahs, however, the Seljuk sultan had defeated the Khwarezmians at the Battle of Yassıçemen that same year.[a] In any case, as a token of gratitude, the benevolent sultan gave Ertugrul and his followers the territories of Karacadag (Karacadağ) near Ankara. Later, after Ertugrul had captured the Karacahisar Castle,[b] the sultan gave the Kayis a new homeland in Domanic (Domaniç) and Sogut,[43] and the vicinity around Bithynia on the eastern borders of Byzantium.[44] From this point onward, the accounts tell us that Ertugrul and his alps spent their winters in Sogut and their summers on the Domanic plateaus which were more suitable for their herds and their nomadic lifestyle.[45] Now the Kayis, among other tribes, were under the protection of the

---

[a] Afyoncu claims that this battle was in fact the Battle of Yassıçemen against Khwarezm Shahs (2020). The Khwarezmians were a Persianate dynasty that ruled parts of the environs in eastern Anatolia.

[b] Some Turkish sources note that the castle was actually captured by Osman I in 1288 CE. If that is indeed the year the castle was captured, its conqueror would have been Osman since by this time, Osman was already a sultan but his father would have fought by his side (Başar, "Ertuğrul Gazi," n.d.).

Seljuk Sultanate of Rum, as they defended the Western frontier of the Seljuk state.[a]

During this period, Seljuk armies were largely composed of *mamluk* and Turkmen soldiers, the latter being less disciplined than the first but were known to be devout supporters of the state and its cause.[46] Stanford Shaw notes that Ertugrul had brought 400 of his followers into the service of the Seljuks of Rum as auxiliaries against the Byzantines and the Mongols.[47] Yet, with the passing of time, the Turkmen tribes slowly established their own principalities in the region, and even became a threat to the declining Byzantine power.[48] Those regional principalities included the Menteşe, Germiyanid, Karasid, Hamidid, and the Sarukhanid in western Anatolia as well as the Çobanoğlu (Chobanid) Beylik in the Black Sea region. Some of these previously established principalities fought against both the Byzantines and the Crusaders, as well as helped settle the oncoming Turkic tribes.[49]

This was not a time of peace for the settlers, and certainly not for Ertugrul and his nascent community. Since their new homeland was right on the borders of the Byzantine Empire, the newcomers often found themselves fending off attacking Crusaders and Mongols, as well as other Turkic tribes and clans fighting and vying for power in the region.[50] Furthermore, leadership of the ummah at this point was at its lowest and provided little to no assistance to other fellow Muslims in need. The Ayyubids in Syria, at least what was left of them, were at odds with the Seljuks, and their ruling elites often allied with their non-Muslim enemies to secretly overthrow one another.[51]

Be that as it may, no such follies distracted the Kayis from their herculean aims. To everyone's astonishment, Ertugrul and

---

[a] Note that after the death of Malik Shah I (r. 1072-1092) the sultan of the Seljuk Empire, the young empire split in two: the Sultanate of Rum to the west and the Seljuk Empire to the east; the first one is often referred to as the Anatolian Seljuk Empire.

his elite warriors brought all of their enemies to their knees; they foiled their traps, defeated their armies, and threw their leaders into disarray. Slowly but surely, many other Turkic tribes accepted Ertugrul as their leader and joined his ranks.[a] At some point, due to his successful military campaigns, Sultan Alaeddin Keykubad even appointed Ertugrul as his regional margrave, a title coveted by many other tribal chieftains.[b] The Turkic sphere of influence began to grow by the day and continued to do so even after the great sultan died and his son Ghiyath al-Din Keykhusrev II (Gıyaseddin) was put in charge of the empire.[52] The young sultan, however, was the last of his line to exercise any significant power.[53]

Ertugrul led the fight to defend his homelands, his faith, and his isolated community until he could do so no more. In his old age, he passed his position of leadership to his son, Osman. It is said that Ertugrul passed away in his 90s in Sogut, in present-day Turkey, where he is also buried. Ertugrul's numerous victories in the region, however, left a vacuum of power in the area and prepared the path for his son, Osman Ghazi,[54] and his followers to build on the foundations laid down by the Kayis and establish one of the longest-lasting empires in world history. This empire, at different points in time, would rule areas of the Middle East, North Africa and Eastern Europe for over 600 years.[55]

---

[a] Notable commanders in the region that joined Ertugrul's cause included Akçakoca, Samsa Çavuş, Kara Tegin, Aykut Alp, and Konur Alp (Afyoncu, 2019).

[b] A margrave was a military governor of a frontier province or *Uç Bey* in Tr., meaning regional head of beys. This was a military title given to semi-autonomous warrior chieftains (Anooshahr, 157, 2009).

The Expeditions of Ertugrul

Do not deceive or be faithless
even with your enemy.

— Abu Bakr as-Saddiq *r.a.*

AVING BEEN RAISED IN HARSH ENVIRONMENTS AND having lived primarily as hunters and herdsmen, most Turkmen children were taught the use of weapons and horsemanship as well as the spirit of warriorship from an early age. Their mastery of these survival skills proved detrimental to their enemies especially when the tribes joined forces with one another.[56] This was Ertugrul's daily life as a child, and his military campaigns during his adulthood exemplified this spirit.

For reasons previously alluded to, it is difficult to know exactly which battles Ertugrul participated in or even when and where. What we know is that ever since the Kayi's settled near Alhat and later in Sogut and Domanic, the nomadic community spent a great deal of their time, energy, and resources in training and battling their adversaries. Moreover, since the Kayis were in the service of the Sultanate of Rum, at least during the leadership of Ertugrul, they often fought the wars of the Seljuks or joined them in their struggles, for which the Kayis were often rewarded.[57]

Ertugrul and his alps, at times together with other tribal chieftains, were often engaged in combat with Mongol and Crusader armies as well as Templars and Byzantines whose borders the Turkic tribes kept testing and pushing further and further.

Although often outnumbered, Ertugrul's ingenious military prowess and tactics proved ruinous to his enemies. Such collective struggles set off a chain of events that greatly weakened Byzantine dominion over the region, and by the time Ertugrul passed away in 1280, he and his alps had established a small state of their own right on the borders of the crumbling Seljuk empire.[58]

The Legacy of Ertugrul

The highest degree in faith is that
you always regard yourself in
the presence of God.

— Uthman ibn Affan *r.a.*

LTHOUGH OFTEN DISPUTED, MANY RESEARCHERS AND HISTORIANS
have concluded that the Ottoman dynasty did in fact
originate from the Kayi tribe.[59] Whatever the case, the
ancestors of the early Ottomans had to have been the people
who settled the region of Bursa, the first major capital city of the
Ottomans, not far from Ertugrul's town of Sogut where Osman
was also born and later established his dynasty. Many Turks today
take pride in such lineage and celebrate that heritage.[60]

The important point to note is that there would not have
been an Ottoman Empire, as we now know it, without the
successful campaigns and efforts of the Kayis and others
who joined their cause. Ertugrul and his alps were the ones
who cleared and paved the way for the rise of the Ottomans
whose empire eventually extended over three continents.[61]
The following are some of the lessons Muslims draw from the life
and legacy of Ertugrul:

- Leadership is best defined as "the art of motivating and influencing people to share a vision of a goal-driven transformational process and to act collaboratively toward its realization."[62] Ertugrul Ghazi did just that. He did not use his position for wealth and power but for the achievement of greater collective goals while influencing others along the way.

- We know that one cannot simply follow another person because of their name, fame, family lineage or wealth, instead the community needs to identify and follow honest and just leaders with a vision firmly grounded in Islamic principles. The Prophet Muhammad *pbuh* has already outlined such principles when it comes to Islamic leadership.[63] Ertugrul, in this case, was elected by the tribal council and led his community by none other than the example of the Prophet Muhammad *pbuh* which he had learned from a very young age.

- Take the best as your example. Looking at the legacy of Ertugrul, we see that it went hand-in-hand with that of his role models: the Prophet Muhammad *pbuh* and his companions, and other later pious Muslim heroes who were the architects of the Muslim civilization.

- Unlike those who work for their own interest alone, Ertugrul was a man with a mission and vision which was to unite the ummah under one banner, that of Islam. He recognized that there is no concept of ummah without unity.

- Like many of his predecessors, he loved and advocated for adherence to justice and fair judgement for all, whether Muslim or non-Muslim.

- He valued honesty and loyalty, and conversely, he despised dishonesty, hypocrisy and disloyalty.

- He learned and embodied the qualities of Islamic leadership as taught in the Qur'an and Sunnah.[64]

- His actions were not to please the people around him but his Creator.

- He was not deceived by great numbers knowing that, as the Qur'an notes, a small group has often overcome a much bigger one.[a]

- Despite all of his preoccupations and life demands, he was and remained a devout person, and taught the same to his family.

- As a commander on the battlefield, he was on the frontlines, not behind the scenes.

- Even if everyone gave up on a cause, he continued alone.

- He was ready to endure hardship and suffering for the sake of his faith, his people, and his cause.

- When faced with challenges and difficulties, instead of acting on his own whims, he consulted the scholars and the experienced.[65]

- Before his death, Ertugrul did not have much to leave behind to his successor, Osman I. He did not leave him any palaces or wealth. Rather, he left him a responsibility—to lead and care for his people, as well as scholars, one of whom was Edibali.

- When Ertugrul died, his life's work did not die with him because during his life he modeled his values for his own progeny who would later shape human history.[66]

- Inspired by his father's vision, his faith, bravery, and kind manners, Osman persistently continued his father's journey, and so did his descendants until their hopes and dreams became a reality.[67]

---

[a] Qur'an 2:249; 8:65.

FINAL REMARKS

I DID NOT WRITE THIS BRIEF BOOK FOR THE SAKE OF WRITING a book. I began researching this book due to my fascination with the historical period discussed here as well as the characters depicted in it. I was perplexed to find out that world history had so little to say about a man and his tribe who clearly were not insignificant in the great scheme of things, at least for the region in question. Those individuals had challenged the status quo, moved through vast territories, traded with people of various backgrounds, coexisted with people of other faiths, made peace alliances and treaties, as well as fought when times called for it. Moreover, from nomadic herdsmen they rose to inconceivable power, came to challenge empires and even established a state of their own. This, I think, deserves a closer look at the people, systems, beliefs, and the context that shaped such struggles and successes. My hope is that there will be more research and translation efforts to shed further light on the topic. For now, unfortunately, this brief work remains the only book on Ertugrul and his tribe that attempts to piece together the scattered paragraphs in history books.

ERTUGRUL'S FAMILY TREE[a]

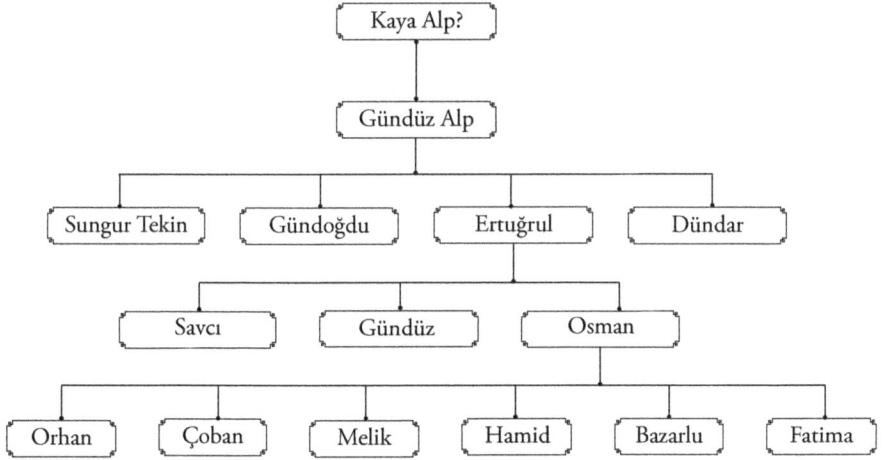

```
                    ┌─────────────┐
                    │  Kaya Alp?  │
                    └─────────────┘
                           │
                    ┌─────────────┐
                    │ Gündüz Alp  │
                    └─────────────┘
         ┌──────────────┬──────────────┬──────────────┐
  ┌─────────────┐ ┌─────────────┐ ┌─────────────┐ ┌─────────────┐
  │ Sungur Tekin│ │  Gündoğdu   │ │  Ertuğrul   │ │   Dündar    │
  └─────────────┘ └─────────────┘ └─────────────┘ └─────────────┘
              ┌──────────────┬──────────────┐
       ┌─────────────┐ ┌─────────────┐ ┌─────────────┐
       │    Savcı    │ │   Gündüz    │ │    Osman    │
       └─────────────┘ └─────────────┘ └─────────────┘
  ┌────────┬────────┬────────┬────────┬────────┐
┌────────┐┌────────┐┌────────┐┌────────┐┌────────┐┌────────┐
│ Orhan  ││ Çoban  ││ Melik  ││ Hamid  ││ Bazarlu││ Fatima │
└────────┘└────────┘└────────┘└────────┘└────────┘└────────┘
```

---

[a] There are numerous family trees listed in İnalcık's research "Osmanlı Beyliği'nin Kurucusu Osman Beg," and most give different names for Ertugrul's grandfather except for three that list Kaya Alp, and that is the one I have preferred since that could be the reason how the Kayi tribe got its name (479–524, 2007).

TIMELINE OF
THE SELJUKS

985 Turkic tribes invade Transoxania[a] and soon after many of them convert to Islam

1037-1063 The reign of Tughrul Bey or Tughril, the founder of the Seljuk Empire

1040 Under the leadership of Tughrul Bey, the Seljuks defeat the Ghaznavids at the Battle of Dandanqan[b]

1042 The Seljuks conquer Khwarezm

1046 Qutalmish, a tribal chieftain and cousin of Tughrul, is sent with an army by Tughrul to force back the Byzantine army at Ganja[c] where he came out victorious

---

[a] Also known as *Ilkhan*.
[b] Year 1038 CE is also cited for this event.
[c] In present-day Azerbaijan.

1048 A number of Turkic tribes raid Byzantine lands for the first time

1054 The Seljuks conquer Iran

1055 The Seljuks under the leadership of Tughrul Bey invade Mesopotamia, overthrow the Shia Buyids there and take over Baghdad; the Abbasid caliph recognizes Turghul Bey as the sultan and temporal ruler of the Muslim state

1063-1072 The reign of Muhammad bin Dawud Chaghri, better known as Alp Arslan, the second sultan of the Seljuk Empire

1064 The Seljuk ruler, Alp Arslan, establishes his capital in Ray, present-day Tehran; Armenia comes under Seljuk rule

1064-1092 The service of Abu Ali Hasan ibn Ali Tusi, known by the title of Nizam al-Mulk. He was a Persian scholar and vizier of the Seljuk Empire. After the assassination of Alp Arslan in 1072, al-Mulk served as the *de facto* ruler of the empire for 20 years

1071 Under Alp Arslan, the Seljuks defeat the Byzantines at the Battle of Manzikert, and capture the Byzantine emperor; Seljuks take over Jerusalem and establish a sultanate in central Anatolia with its capital in Nicaea, present-day Iznik

1073 Seljuks defeat the Qarakhanids; they take Bukhara and Samarkand

1076 Seljuks take Syria and Palestine

1077 Suleiman ibn Qutalmish founds a new state, the Sultanate of Rum (also known as the Seljuks of Anatolia) in western Anatolia.

Although initially a vassal of the Great Seljuk Empire, it later becomes and independent sultanate

1086 Seliuks take Antioch and Aleppo

1092 The Great Seljuk Empire and the Sultanate of Rum officially split into two separate Seljuk empires

1092-1107 The reign of Kilij Arslan I (of the Seljuk Sultanate of Rum) based first in Nicaea (Iznik) and later Konya[a]

1096 The Seljuks of Rum under Kilij Arslan I annihilate the Pope's Crusade

1097 Crusaders take Nicaea (Iznik). That same year Crusaders defeat the Seljuks of Rum at Dorylaeum (Eskişehir)

1099 Crusaders under the leadership of Emperor Frederick Barbarossa attack Konya

1171 Salah al-Din Ayyubbid ends the Fatimid dynasty in Egypt and founds the Ayyubid dynasty

1198 Ertugrul, son of Gunduz Alp and father of Osman I, is born[b]

Ca. 1200s During the first part of the century under the leadership of Gündüz Alp, the father of Ertugrul, the Kayi tribe settles in the

---

[a] Just recently, Turkish archeologists from Dicle University discovered Sultan Kilij Arslan's grave in southeast Turkey (Gershon, "Turkish Archeologists Discover Grave...," 2021).
[b] As mentioned earlier, year 1191 CE is also cited for this event but both dates are disputed.

eastern province of Bitlis in Anatolia now under the control of the Sultanate of Rum

1210-1220 The reign of Keykaus I or Keykavus I of the Seljuk Sultanate of Rum[a]

1220-1237 The reign of Sultan Alaeddin Keyqubad I of the Seljuk Sultanate of Rum.[b] Keyqubad I is known to have formed alliances with the Ayyubids in Syria in order to prevent the expansion of the Khwarazm Shahs in the region who had greatly reduced the influence of the Great Seljuks and were engaged in attempts to overthrow the Abbasid Caliphate

1230 Ertugrul and his alps assist Sultan Alaeddin Keyqubad on the battlefield and defeat the sultan's enemies. In return, the sultan gives the Kayis lands near Ankara and later a new homeland in Sogut and Domanic

1231 Ertugrul and his alps capture the Karacahisar Castle from the Byzantines which greatly strengthens the positions of the Kayis in the region[c]

1237-1246 The reign of Ghiyath al-Din Keykhusrev II or Keykhusraw II of the Seljuk Sultanate of Rum

1243 The army of Keykhusraw II of the Seljuks of Rum is defeated by the Mongols at the Battle of Kose Dagh (Köse Dağ). Although the sultan was allowed to keep his throne in Konya, from that point

---

[a] Year 1211 CE is also found for the beginning of Keykaus's rule.
[b] Year 1219 CE is also found for the beginning of Keyqubad's rule.
[c] Year 1232 CE is also cited for this event.

on he became a vassal of the Mongols and paid them tribute. Due to this fracture of Seljuk control, a number of beyliks emerged in the region[68]

1249-1257 The reign of Sultan Alaeddin Keyqubad II of the Seljuk Sultanate of Rum

1258 Osman I, son of Ertugrul, is born in Sogut; Mongol armies sack Baghdad, massaker its population and kill the caliph

1269-1310 The foundation of the ghazi principalities of Aydin, Menteşe, Saruhan, Karesi and later Ottoman in western Anatolia.

1280 Ertugrul, son of Gunduz Alp, dies in Sogut[a]

1292-1302 The reign of Sultan Alaeddin Keyqubad III of the Seljuk Sultanate of Rum, although his reign was intermittent due to his unpopularity[b]

1299 The descendants of Ertugrul give rise to the Ottoman dynasty

1302 The Ottomans, under the leadership of Osman I defeat the Byzantines at the Battle of Bapheus. This victory cements the Ottoman state and heralds the final capture of Bithynia[69]

1307 After the lands of the Sultanate of Rum were curved up between the quarreling sons of Sultan Keykhusraw II, Seljuk territories became an Ilkhanid province

---

[a] Due to historical gaps and discrepancies, the exact dates of Ertugrul's birth and death are difficult to confirm but some sources also indicate 1281 CE as the year when Ertugrul passed away.

[b] Years 1284, 1292-3, 1301-3 are also found for the timeframes of his rule.

GLOSSARY OF TERMS, NAMES, AND PLACES

Alp: hero, brave one, chivalrous, etc., and/or soldier

Allah: the Arabic word for the one and only God; a term also used by non-Muslim Arabic speaker

Arab: a person originally from the Arabian peninsula and the neighboring territories, inhabiting much of the Middle East, North Africa and beyond

Bey: ruler of an independent principality, prince or governor of a district

Caliph: leader of the Muslim community and successor of the Prophet Muhammad *pbuh*; vicegerent

Clan: a large family or a group of close-knit and interrelated families (usually from a tribe)

Sahaba: Arabic for Companions of the Prophet Muhammad, the founding generation of Muslims who knew, met, and lived with the Prophet *pbuh*

Emir: from the Arabic word *amir* for 'prince' or 'one who commands'; a Turkish title designating a military commander

Hadith: a recorded tradition of the sayings and actions of the Prophet Muhammad *pbuh*

Hijra: the emigration of the Prophet Muhammad *pbuh* from Makkah to Madinah in 622 CE; the start of the Muslim calendar

Imam: the leader of the Muslim community; the one who leads the prayers

Iman: faith or belief

Islam: the faith of the Muslims, and world's second-largest religion

Madinah: an old city in western Saudi Arabia, also known and the City of the Prophet

Makkah: a city in Saudi Arabia, also known as the birthplace of the Prophet *pbuh* and the holiest city of Islam

Mamluk: from the Arabic word referring to slave-soldiers

Messenger: a person who carries and/or delivers a message or information

Muslim: a follower of the religion of Islam; one who submits to the will of God

Prophet: a person regarded as an inspired teacher, messenger, or proclaimer of God's words, in this case Prophet Muhammad *pbuh*

Rum: The Arabic word for 'Romans' referring to the Byzantines (the Eastern Christians) or often to Westerners in general

Seljuk: a Turkic dynasty that established itself in Persia in the 11th century and moved westward toward Anatolia

Sultanate: a state or domain governed by a sultan

Sunni: an orthodox Muslim

Tribe: a group of people consisting of families and/or clans and linked together by social, religious, or blood ties, often having a common culture and a recognized leader. Tribes, like clans, are often united by actual or perceived ties of kinship and ancestry

Turkmen: Turkic nomads who moved from western Central Asia and travelled through the lands of Anatolia, and even settled there, with their families and flocks. They were known for great skills such as horse-archery, among others

Ummah: the Muslim community as a whole

Vezir: from the Arabic word *wazir* for minister or the one in charge of the administration of the realm in the name of the caliph

APPENDIX A: TRANSLITERATION CHART

Letters	Read as (IPA)[a]	Pronounced as	English equivalent
A a	/aː/	/a/	aunt
B b	/beː/	/b/	bank
C c	/d͡ʒeː/	/d͡ʒ/	gem
Ç ç	/t͡ʃeː/	/t͡ʃ/	chant
D d	/deː/	/d/	door
E e	/eː/	/e/	rent
F f	/feː/	/f/	fat
G g	/ɟeː/	/g/, /ɟ/	goal
Ğ ğ	soft G (often silent)	/ɰ/	brougham
H h	/heː/ or /haː/	/h/	hat
I ı	/ɯː/	/ɯ/	Moses
İ i	/iː/	/i/	see
J j	/ʒeː/	/ʒ/	pleasure
K k	/ceː/ or /kaː/	/k/, /c/	kid
L l	/leː/	/ɫ/, /l/	live
M m	/meː/	/m/	milk
N n	/neː/	/n/	nine
O o	/oː/	/o/	more
Ö ö	/œː/	/œ/	Norse
P p	/peː/	/p/	pen
R r	/ɾeː/	/ɾ/	red
S s	/seː/	/s/	sad
Ş ş	/ʃeː/	/ʃ/	shot
T t	/teː/	/t/	ten
U u	/uː/	/u/	zoo
Ü ü	/yː/	/y/	'as in French 'tu
V v	/veː/	/v/	vest
Y y	/jeː/	/j/	yet
Z z	/zeː/	/z/	zebra

---

[a] International Phonetic Alphabet.

APPENDIX B: PORTRAITS

Traditional Ertugrul Ghazi portrait by Derviş Mehmed.[70]

Modern Ertugrul Ghazi portrait inspired by
the 'Resurrection: Ertugrul' series.
Art by Lama Bayoun, 2020.

◇〉———〈◇

ACKNOWLEDGMENTS

I am deeply grateful to everyone who took the time to read this humble work and shared their invaluable feedback with me, especially Marisa Petersen, Andrea Lowgren, Stef Keris, Omar Reda, Amber Haque, Burhan Fili, Didmar Faja, Erzen Pashaj, Amjad Hussain, Brandon Mayfield, Naser Bresa, Paul Fattig, Maqsood Chaudhary, Jetmir Ahmeti, Tom McLaughlin, and many more. Their critiques have inspired me, and have greatly enriched the book at hand.

A special thanks to my parents, siblings and relatives who have always supported my work. You all inspire me. Thank you even if I did not mention you by name.

◈§——⸰§◈

BIBLIOGRAPHY

Afyoncu, Erhan. "Ertuğrul Gazi ve Karakeçili Şenlikleri."
    Ahaber. 8 Sept. 2019, https://www.ahaber.com.tr/yazarlar/
    erhan-afyoncu/2019/09/08/ertugrul-gazi-ve-karakecili-
    senlikleri. Accessed 4 Nov. 2020.

____. *Herkes İçin Kısa Osmanlı Tarihi: (1302 - 1922)*. Istanbul,
    Yeditepe Yayınevi, 2017.

___. *Ottoman Empire Unveiled*. Istanbul, Yeditepe Yayınevi,
    2012.

___. *Sorularla Osmanlı İmparatorluğu*. Istanbul, Yeditepe
    Yayınevi, 2016.

___. "The Story of Ertuğrul Gazi's Tomb." *Daily Sabah*, 2020
    https://www.dailysabah.com/opinion/op-ed/the-story-of-
    ertugrul-gazis-tomb. Accessed 4 Nov. 2020.

Akgunduz, Ahmed, and Said Ozturk. *Ottoman History -
    Misperceptions and Truths*. IUR Press, 2011.

Al-Hassani, Salim. *1001 Inventions: The Enduring Legacy
    of Muslim Civilization*. Washington, D.C, National
    Geographic, 2012.

Al-Salaabi, Ali Muhammad. *Sultan Muhammad Al-Fatih*.
    London, All-Firdous, 2008.

Ansary, Tamim. *The Invention of Yesterday: A 50,000-Year History of Human Culture, Conflict, and Connection.* New York, PublicAffairs, 2019.

Anooshahr, Ali. *The Ghazi Sultans and the Frontiers of Islam: A Comparative Study of the Late Medieval and Early Modern Periods.* London, Routledge, 2009.

Armstrong, Karen. *Islam: A Short History.* New York, Modern Library, 2000.

Arnold, Thomas. *The Spread of Islam in the World: A History of Peaceful Preaching.* New Delhi, Goodword Books, 2003.

Artuk, Ibrahim. "Osmanlı Beyliği'nin Kurucusu Osman Gazi'ye Ait Sikke." Türkiye'nin Sosyal ve Ekonomik Tarihi: 1071-1920, 1980, pp. 27-31.

Barber, Malcolm. *Crusader States.* Yale University Press, 2012.

Başar, Fahameddin. "Ertuğrul Gazi." *TDV İslam Ansiklopedisi,* Türkiye Diyanet Vakfı, islamansiklopedisi.org.tr/ ertugrul-gazi. Accessed 21 Dec. 2020.

Beekun, Rafik and Jamal A Badawi. *Leadership: An Islamic Perspective.* Beltsville, Amana Publications, 1999.

Christie, Niall. *Muslims and Crusaders.* London, Routledge, 2014.

Cahen, Claude. "Keyhusrev II." *Encyclopaedia of Islam,* Ed. by Peri Bearman, Brill, 2007.

DeWeese, Devin. *Islamization and Native Religion in the Golden Horde: Baba Tükles and Conversion to Islam in Historical and Epic Tradition.* University Park, Pennsylvania, The Pennsylvania State University Press, 2007.

Findley, Carter. *The Turks in World History.* Oxford Etc., Oxford University Press, 2005.

Finkel, Caroline. *Osman's Dream: The Story of the Ottoman Empire, 1300-1923.* New York, Basic Books, 2005.

Frashëri, Sami. *The Expansion of Islam: A Nineteenth Century Treatise*. Oregon, Independently published, 2019.

Frazier, Ian. "Invaders: Destroying Baghdad." *The New Yorker*, 17 Apr. 2005, www.newyorker.com/magazine/2005/04/25/invaders-3. Accessed 30 Oct. 2020.

Gershon, Livia. "Turkish Archaeologists Discover Grave of Sultan Who Defeated Crusaders." *Smithsonian*, 14 Jan. 2021. *SmartNews*, www.smithsonianmag.com/smart-news/grave-sultan-who-defeated-crusaders-uncovered-180976761/?fbclid=IwAR26FvkdBpkmqgT7vKuptoue7i6v4LFxyh3bhfRl5h5jo-gZbiabilNpISc. Accessed 15 Jan. 2021.

Goodwin, Jason. *Lords of the Horizons*. New York, Owl Books, 1998.

Hayward, Joel. "Revisiting the Past: The Value of Teaching Islamic Military History." *Cambridge Muslim College Papers*, Series 8, 2020, 479141-1506839-raikfcquaxqnco fqfm.stackpathdns.com/wp-content/uploads/2020/10/CMC-paper-Joel-C.pdf.

___. *The Leadership of Muhammad*. Claritas Books, 2021.

Howard, Douglas A. *A History of the Ottoman Empire*. Cambridge University Press, 2017.

Ibnü'l-Verdi. *Selçuklular*. Translated by Mustafa Alican, Istanbul, Kronik Kitap, 2017.

İnalcık, Halil. "Osmanlı Beyliği'nin Kurucusu Osman Beg." *Belleten*, vol. 7, no. 261, 2007, pp. 480–490.

___. *The Ottoman Empire and Europe: The Ottoman Empire and Its Place in European History*. Istanbul, Kronik Kitap, 2017.

___. *The Ottoman Empire. The Classical Age*. New York: Aristide D.Caratzas, 1973.

___. *The Ottoman Empire: Sultan Society and Economy*. Istanbul, Kronik Kitap, 2018.

Kafadar, Cemal. *Between Two Worlds: The Construction of the Ottoman State*. Berkeley, University of California Press, 1995.

Kinross, Lord. *The Ottoman Centuries: The Rise and Fall of the Turkish Empire*. New York, Morrow Quill, 1977.

Köymen, Mehmet. *Büyük Alâeddîn Keykubad ve Zamanı*. Istanbul, Kronik Kitap, 2020.

Küçüksipahioğlu, Birsel. "The First Turkish Leader against the Crusaders: Sultan Kilij Arslan." Şarkiyat Mecmuası, no. 1, 2015, pp. 63–83, dergipark.org.tr/tr/download/article-file/496563. Accessed 10 Jan. 2021.

Lindner, Rudi. *Explorations in Ottoman Prehistory*. Ann Arbor, University Of Michigan Press, 2007, babel.hathitrust.org/cgi/pt?id=mdp.39015066874515&view=1up&seq=13. Accessed 21 Dec. 2020.

___. *Nomads and Ottomans in Medieval Anatolia*. Richmond, Curzon Press, 1997.

Maalouf, Amin. *The Crusades through Arab Eyes*. translated by Jon Rothschild, London, Al Saqi Books, 1984.

McCarthy, Justin. *The Ottoman Turks*. Routledge, 1997.

Mikhail, Alan. *God's Shadow: Sultan Selim, His Ottoman Empire, and the Making of the Modern World*. New York, NY, Liveright Publishing Corporation, 2020.

Riley-Smith, Jonathan. *The Crusades: A History*. 2nd ed., Yale University Press, 2005.

Romero, Libby. *Ibn Al-Haytham: The Man Who Discovered How We See*. National Geographic, 2016.

Runciman, Steven. *The First Crusade*. New York, Cambridge University Press, 2005.

Usta, Aydin. *Selçuklu Sultanları*. Istanbul, Yeditepe Yayınevi, 2019.

___. *Sorularla Selcuklu Devleti*. Istanbul, Yeditepe Yayinevi, 2020.

Scaruffi, Piero. *A Time-Line of the Turks*. Scaruffi, 1999, www. scaruffi.com/politics/turks.html. Accessed 22 Oct. 2020.

Shaw, Stanford J. *History of the Ottoman Empire and Modern Turkey*. Vol. 1, Cambridge, Cambridge University Press, 1976.

Stiker, Martin. *The Islamic World in Ascendancy: From the Arab Conquests to the Siege of Vienna*. Greenwood Publishing, 2000.

Sümer, Faruk. "Kayı." *TDV İslam Ansiklopedisi*, Türkiye Diyanet Vakfı, islamansiklopedisi.org.tr/kayi. Accessed 20 Dec. 2020.

Şimşiroğlu, Ahmet. *Kayı I: Ertuğrul'un Ocağı*. İstanbul, Timaş Yayınları, 2013.

Tezcan, Baki. *The Second Ottoman Empire Political and Social Transformation in the Early Modern World*. Cambridge Cambridge University Press, 2010.

The Cambridge History of Turkey, Ed. by Kate Fleet, vol. 1, Cambridge, Cambridge University Press, 2009.

Topbaş, Osman N. *Osmanet: Me Personalitetet Dhe Institucionet E Tyre Monumentale*. Progresi, 2009.

Weir, William. *50 Battles That Changed the World: The Conflicts That Most Influenced the Course Of History*. New Jersey, New Page, 2004.

Wells, H G. *The Outline of History*. New York, Garden City Books, 1961.

Yilmaz, Yakup. "Osmanlıların Kuruluşuna Dair İkilemler." *Journal of History and Future*, vol. 1, 1, Dec. 2015, p.

8–38,https://dergipark.org.tr/tr/download/article-file/176830.

Yorulmazoglu, Erol. *The Turks: The Central Asian Civilization That Bridged the East and West for over Two Millennia*. Vol. 1, North Carolina, Create Space, 2017.

Zachariadou, Elizabeth. "Turkomans." *The Oxford Dictionary of Byzantium*, Ed. by Alexander Kazhdan, Oxford University Press, 1991.

ABOUT THE AUTHOR

FLAMUR VEHAPI is a researcher, chronologist, poet, literary translator, academic, and a success coach. He received his B.S. in Counseling Psychology with a minor in History from Southern Oregon University, and his M.A. in Conflict Resolution from Portland State University. Currently, he is an Education and Leadership PhD student at Pacific University. In 2009, Vehapi received the *Imagine Award* for Community Peacemaking. He taught social sciences at Rogue Community College and Southern Oregon University, after which he taught at various institutions in the Middle East. He has authored several books and translated two of Sami Frashëri's works. He has worked as a contributing writer for the PSU Chronicles. Vehapi and his family currently live in Oregon.

NOTES

1   Topbaş, *Osmanet: Me Personalitetet Dhe Institucionet E Tyre Monumentale*, 19, 2009. Cf. Afyoncu, *Herkes İçin Kısa Osmanlı Tarihi: (1302 - 1922)*, 2017; İnalcık, *The Ottoman Empire*, 1973.

2   The Historical Atlas by William R. Shepherd, 1911. From Wikimedia   Commons.

3   Lindner, *Explorations in Ottoman Prehistory*, 1, 2007. Cf. Afyoncu, *Ottoman Empire Unveiled*, 2012; Mikhail, *God's Shadow*, 2020; İnalcık, *The Ottoman Empire and Europe*, 2017.

4   Başar, "Ertuğrul Gazi." *TDV İslam Ansiklopedisi*, n.d. According to Afyoncu, through their invaluable works, historians like Mükrimin Halil Yinanç, Fahamettin Başar, Ismail Hakkı Konyalı, and Tayyip Gökbilgin compiled the most details about Ertugrul and his tribe (2020).

5   Personal translations.

6   Cf. Al-Hassani, *1001 Inventions*, 2012; Romero, *Ibn Al-Haytham*, 2016.

7   Cf. Al-Hassani, *1001 Inventions*, 2012.

8   Cf. Armstrong, *Islam*, 2000; Frazier, "Invaders: Destroying Baghdad," 2005.

9   Cf. Afyoncu, *Sorularla Osmanlı İmparatorluğu*, 2016.

10 Cf. Frazier, "Invaders: Destroying Baghdad," 2005.

11 As qtd. in Al-Salaabi, *Sultan Muhammad Al-Fatih*, 27, 2008.

12 Maalouf, *The Crusades through Arab Eyes*, 235-246, 1984. Cf. Armstrong, *Islam*, 2000; Al-Salaabi, *Sultan Muhammad Al-Fatih*, 2008.

13 For more on the ways of the nomads, see Lindner, *Nomads and Ottomans in Medieval Anatolia*, 1997; Yorulmazoglu, *The Turks* (vol. 1), 2017; Ansary, *The Invention of Yesterday*, 196-202, 2019, and pass.

14 Kinross, *The Ottoman Centuries*, 15-16, 1977; Wells, *The Outline of History*, 567-569, 1961.

15 Cf. Arnold, *The Spread of Islam...*, 2003; Frashëri, *The Expansion of Islam*, 2019.

16 Shaw, *History of the Ottoman Empire and Modern Turkey*, vol. 1, 3-4, 1976.

17 Christie, *Muslims and Crusaders,* 8, 2014. Cf. McCarthy, *The Ottoman Turks,* 6-8; 1997; Findley, *The Turks in World History,* 50, 2005; Shaw, *History of the Ottoman Empire and Modern Turkey,* vol. 1, 1976; DeWeese, *Islamization and Native Religion in the Golden Horde,* 2007.

18 Kinross, *The Ottoman Centuries,* 16, 1977.

19 Christie, *Muslims and Crusaders,* 8, 2014; Armstrong, *Islam,* 81, 2000; Kinross, *The Ottoman Centuries,*16, 1977; Shaw, *History of the Ottoman Empire and Modern Turkey,* vol. 1, 4-6, 1976.

20 Cf. *The Cambridge History of Turkey,* ed. by Kate Fleet, vol. 1, 6-50 2009, and pass.

21 Cf. Usta, *Sorularla Selcuklu Devleti,* 2020; Ibnü'l-Verdi, *Selçuklular* (Trans. by Mustafa Alican), 2017.

22 Shaw, *History of the Ottoman Empire and Modern Turkey,* vol. 1, 4-5, 1976; Runciman, *The First Crusade,* 27, 2005. Cf. McCarthy, *The Ottoman Turks,* 1997.

23 Christie, *Muslims and Crusaders,* 8, 2014; Kinross, *The Ottoman Centuries,* 18, 1977.

24 Barber, *Crusader States,* 9, 2012; Wells, *The Outline of History,* 567-569, 1961.

25 Runciman, The First Crusade, 28, 2005; Weir, 50 Battles That Changed the World, 293, 2004; Armstrong, Islam, 95, 2000

26 Cf. Lindner, *Explorations in Ottoman Prehistory,* 2-15, 2007.

27 Lindner, *Explorations in Ottoman Prehistory,* 3, 2007.

28 Cf. Köymen, *Büyük Alâeddîn Keykubad ve Zamanı,* 2020.

29 Lindner, *Explorations in Ottoman Prehistory,* 3, 2007.

30 Sümer, "Kayı." TDV İslam Ansiklopedisi, n.d.; Findley, *The Turks in World History,* 50, 2005.

31 Afyoncu, "Ertuğrul Gazi ve Karakeçili şenlikleri", 2019.

32 Akgunduz & Ozturk, Ottoman History, 35, 2011.

33 Kafadar, *Between Two Worlds,* 185, 1995.

34 Cf. Topbaş, Osmanet: *Me Personalitetet Dhe Institucionet E Tyre Monumentale,* 19, 2009.

35 f. Yilmaz, "Osmanlıların Kuruluşuna…" 8-38, 2015; Akgunduz and Ozturk, *Ottoman History,* 35, 2011; Howard, *A History of the Ottoman Empire,* 2017; Başar, "Ertuğrul Gazi." *TDV İslam Ansiklopedisi,* n.d.

36 Cf. Topbaş, Osmanet: *Me Personalitetet Dhe Institucionet E Tyre Monumentale,* 19-20, 2009; Al-Salaabi, *Sultan Muhammad Al-Fatih,* 2008.

37 Al-Salaabi, *Sultan Muhammad Al-Fatih,* 25, 2008; Shaw, *History of the Ottoman Empire and Modern Turkey,* vol. 1, 13, 1976. Ahlat is located in East Turkey near Lake Van (Ar. Wa'an).

38 Lindner, *Explorations in Ottoman Prehistory,* 1, 2007. Cf. McCarthy, *The Ottoman Turks,* 1997.

39 Cf. *The Cambridge History of Turkey,* ed. by Kate Fleet, vol. 1, 51-101, 2009, and pass.

40 Afyoncu, "The Story of Ertuğrul…" 2020; Başar, "Ertuğrul Gazi." *TDV İslam Ansiklopedisi,* n.d.

41 Al-Salaabi, *Sultan Muhammad Al-Fatih,* 25, 2008; Shaw, *History of the Ottoman Empire and Modern Turkey,* vol. 1, 13, 1976.

42 Some sources indicate that this was a Christian Byzantine army (Al-Salaabi, 26, 2008). Cf. Usta, *Selçuklu Sultanları, 2019;* Köymen, *Büyük Alâeddîn Keykubad ve Zamanı,* 2020.

43 Başar, "Ertuğrul Gazi." *TDV İslam Ansiklopedisi,* n.d.

44 Shaw, *History of the Ottoman Empire and Modern Turkey,* vol. 1, 13, 1976. Cf. Finkel, 7, 2005; Afyoncu, "The Story of Ertuğrul…" 2020; Başar, "Ertuğrul Gazi." *TDV İslam Ansiklopedisi,* n.d.

45 Başar, "Ertuğrul Gazi." TDV *İslam Ansiklopedisi,* n.d.

46 Christie, *Muslims and Crusaders,* 8, 2014.

47 Shaw, *History of the Ottoman Empire and Modern Turkey,* vol. 1, 13, 1976.

48 Goodwin, *Lords of the Horizons,* 7, 1998; İnalcık, *The Ottoman Empire,* 5-6, 1973; Kinross, *The Ottoman Centuries,* 17, 1977; Wells, *The Outline of History,* 567-569, 1961.

49 Afyoncu, "The Story of Ertuğrul…" 2020.

50 Cf. Finkel, *Osman's Dream,* 2005.

51 Runciman, *The First Crusade,* 32, 2005.

52 Cf. Köymen, *Büyük Alâeddîn Keykubad ve Zamanı,* 2020

53 Cahen, 748, 2007.

54 Riley-Smith, *The Crusades: A History,* 270, 2005. Cf. Finkel, *Osman's Dream,* 2005.

55 Afyoncu, *Ottoman Empire Unveiled,* 11, 2012. Cf. İnalcık, *The Ottoman Empire and Europe,* 2017; Afyoncu, *Herkes İçin Kısa Osmanlı Tarihi: (1302 - 1922),* 2017.

56 Cf. McCarthy, *The Ottoman Turks,* 1997.

57 Cf. Shaw, *History of the Ottoman Empire and Modern Turkey,* vol. 1, 13, 1976; Afyoncu, "Ertuğrul Gazi ve Karakeçili şenlikleri," 2019.

58 Riley-Smith, *The Crusades: A History,* 270, 2005. Cf. Finkel, *Osman's Dream,* 2005.

59 Findley, *The Turks in World History,* 50, 2005. Cf. Afyoncu, "The Story of Ertuğrul…," 2020.

60 Afyoncu, "Ertuğrul Gazi ve Karakeçili şenlikleri," 2019.

61 Cf. Afyoncu, *Sorularla Osmanlı İmparatorluğu,* 2016.

62 Hayward, "Revisiting the Past: The Value of Teaching Islamic Military History," 5, 2020.

63 Cf. Hayward, *The Leadership of Muhammad,* 2021.

64 For more on this topic, see *Leadership: An Islamic Perspective* by Beekun and Badawi, 1999; Hayward, "Revisiting the Past...," 2020.

65 Cf. Al-Salaabi, *Sultan Muhammad Al-Fatih,* 36-70, 2008

66 Cf. Al-Salaabi, *Sultan Muhammad Al-Fatih,* 30-35, 2008.

67 C.f İnalcık, *The Ottoman Empire: Sultan Society and Economy,* 2018. Cf. Afyoncu's *Herkes İçin Kısa Osmanlı Tarihi: (1302 - 1922),* 2017.

68 Cf. *The Cambridge History of Turkey,* ed. by Kate Fleet, vol. 1, 2009.

69 Cf. İnalcık, *The Ottoman Empire: Sultan Society and Economy,* 2018.

70 Public domain from Wikimedia Commons, 2020.

Other Titles by Crescent Books

The World According to Sami Frashëri by Flamur Vehapi, 2024

The Spectacular Escape by Burhan Al-Din Fili, 2023

Atheism Versus Belief by Brandon Mayfield, 2023

Kosovo: A Brief Chronology by Flamur Vehapi, 2023

Verses of the Heart: Poems by Flamur Vehapi, 2021

Crescent Books

Ertugrul Ghazi
A Very Short Biography

by Flamur Vehapi
with a Foreword by Dr. Stef Keris

First Published in 2021, by Crescent Books
an imprint of Crescent Institute LLC
Portland, OR

ISBN: 978-1-954935-00-6

1. Ertugrul   2. Byzantines   3. Mongols
4. Crusaders   5. Sultan Alaeddin
6. Ottomans   7. Turkmen